The Life of
SAINT
MACRINA

BY GREGORY, BISHOP OF NYSSA

Translated, with introduction and notes,
by Kevin Corrigan

Wipf & Stock
PUBLISHERS
Eugene, Oregon

Wipf and Stock Publishers
199 W 8th Ave, Suite 3
Eugene, OR 97401

The Life of Saint Macrina
By Gregory, Bishop of Nyssa and Corrigan, Kevin
Copyright©2001 Peregrina Publishing Co.
ISBN: 1-59752-389-5
Publication date: 8/10/2005
Previously published by Peregrina Publishing Co., 2001

CONTENTS

INTRODUCTION

The *Life of Saint Macrina* [VSM],[1] written sometime between A.D. 380 and 383, is the story of a remarkable woman and a remarkable family. It is told by her younger brother, Gregory, who at the time of writing was certainly not aware that he too was to become a celebrated saint.

The eldest of ten children,[2] Macrina was born – probably in 327 A.D. – into a long-established and wealthy Cappadocian family, whose deep commitment to Christianity had been tried and tested in the savage persecutions of Diocletian when Macrina's grandparents had had to flee for safety to the mountains of Pontus. Her maternal grandfather had even lost his life and all his possessions on account of his opposition to the emperor; and yet, as she tells us herself in the VSM (p. 18), the family was always blessed by God because of their enduring faith. Of this blessing, wealth seems to have played the lesser part. Her paternal grandmother was St. Macrina the Elder, the follower of another saint, the legendary Gregory Thaumaturgus ("Wonderworker") who had been bishop of Neo-Caesarea in Pontus.

Macrina's parents were St. Basil and St. Emmelia, the father a rhetorician of distinction in his own land, the mother, Macrina's life-long friend and companion, a very human figure in the portrait given us by Gregory in the VSM. And although her father died at a comparatively early age (in 340 when Macrina was only twelve years old), the witness of his caring for the poor, his hospitality, the purity of his life, his generosity to the church and, above all, his devotion to prayer, was to live on in his family and in the lives of his children.[3]

Of Macrina's sisters we know nothing. Of her brothers three were to become famous bishops: St. Basil of Caesarea, St. Gregory of Nyssa and St. Peter of Sebaste and two – Basil and Peter – were to found a monastic tradition and to be leaders of monastic communities. Macrina and Peter founded a convent and monastery respectively close by each other on the banks of the river Iris, while Basil's monastery was probably located on the opposite bank. A fourth brother, Naucratius rejected a brilliant career in rhetoric at the age of twenty-one and withdrew to a remote part of the country where he lived a life of prayer and poverty caring for the aged and the sick until he was accidentally killed in a hunting accident while procuring food for those in his care.

As for the family's friends, the best friend of Basil's student years was to be no less than the third great Cappadocian Father, St. Gregory of Nazianzus, bishop of Constantinople and, together with St. Basil and St. Gregory in Cappadocia, St. Athanasius in Egypt, theologian and defender of the Nicene faith against the overwhelming power of the Arian heresy in the fourth century.

In the VSM we receive a personal account of what it was like to live amid this constellation of saints. Gregory's portrait of Macrina is sometimes idealised, it is true, and we can have no means of discerning in certain passages what is true to fact and what has been added as a result of reflection and the writer's art. But, just as in the case of Plato and his revered historical Socrates, so in Gregory's portrait of his eldest sister the genuinely human face of the great Macrina shines out to us across the centuries. As a result, a major influence in the history of Christianity begins to emerge, an influence surely eclipsed but for Gregory's tribute.

Macrina was born in 327, then Basil in 329, then Naucratius, followed by Gregory in 331 or later, down to Peter, the youngest child, in 341. Their father died in 340, and there is no doubt from

Gregory's account that Macrina, though only twelve years old, was the major pillar of strength for the family at this time. Although Basil himself does not speak of her, Gregory, only four years her junior, calls her his teacher (διδάσκαλος) and tells us that when Peter was born, Macrina personally took his education in hand and became everything for the child: "father, teacher, guide, mother." Her strength of resolve and religious devotion had, in fact, been demonstrated even before the death of her father, after the unexpected death of her fiancé; for against her parents' wishes, something unique in early accounts of saints' lives,[4] she determined to remain unmarried, and never to separate herself from her mother, but to live a life of asceticism. At a very early age, then, she recited the psalms at appropriate times during the day and was not only skilled in the genteel task of spinning, but also insisted upon performing the servile one of preparing bread for her mother "with her own hands." This is the girl who grows up as the partner to her mother's worries, persuades her mother to turn the family home into a monastery, to hold all possessions "in common" and to treat her maids as "sisters and equals instead of slaves and servants," who with her mother founds the convent at Annisa by the Iris (probably in 352) and who gives all her possessions away when her mother dies in 370. And this too is the girl who, according to Gregory's testimony, takes Basil in hand when he comes home from university "monstrously conceited about his skill in rhetoric, contemptuous of every high reputation and exalted beyond the leading lights of the province by his self-importance," ultimately to win him to "the ideal of philosophy."

I am not suggesting that Macrina is responsible *simpliciter* for Basilian monasticism or even that she was the first to adopt a true monastic spirit in her own home. Undoubtedly, Basil must also have influenced Macrina as she obviously influenced him. Indeed too, the importance of women in the establishment and direction of monasteries is already in evidence at this time. Pachomius entrusted his sister with the direction of a convent. According to Athanasius, the sister of Anthony was in charge of a monastery in Egypt.[5] And in a letter of Jerome we read that at Rome in about 350, a widow Marcella transformed her house into a convent; and similar things happened elsewhere, in Palestine, Spain, Gaul, Africa and Italy.[6] Nonetheless, it is important to see that in Macrina, as also in her mother, Emmelia, we see a major guiding, and undoubtedly creative, force in the development of monasticism. Whether or not Macrina was a deaconess, and there seems no evidence to suggest that she was, her influence upon the major currents of her own time is evident on almost every page of the VSM, an influence which goes to the very heart of Christianity, the hidden humanising life of renunciation which Gregory will not permit to "pass along this way veiled and in silence" (p. 18).

THE FOURTH CENTURY

THE HUMAN FACES OF GREGORY & MACRINA

Macrina and Gregory lived in a century which had seen the persecutions of Diocletian, and the conversion of Constantine and the replacement of the "immortal gods of Rome." It had also witnessed the preaching of a north African priest, Arius (c. 250–336), and the spread of a doctrine which maintained inter alia that the Son of God was subordinate to the Father, created out of nothing as an instrument for the creation of the world. Sixteen hundred years later we may find it hard to take many of the details of these intricate debates about the nature of Christ and the Trinity too seriously. Nevertheless, these debates were of enormous importance to the development of, and indeed first of all to the survival of Christianity. The great councils of the period, especially the Council of Nicaea in 325, and in the next century the council of Chalcedon which met in 451, were not attempting to define sacred mysteries, but rather to find adequate and proper ways of speaking about those mysteries, ways which would honestly reflect scripture and tradition, and which would not ultimately result in destroying the very faith they were trying to illuminate. This is what lay at the root of the sometimes vicious and violent struggle between Arianism and Orthodoxy in the fourth century. St. Athanasius' patriarchy was particularly stormy. Out of the forty-five years Athanasius was Archbishop of Alexandria, he spent seventeen of them in exile. Similar difficulties, if not quite so extreme, assailed the great Cappadocian Fathers; and in the VSM we get an unusual glimpse behind the scenes, as it were, at the beleaguered bishop of the time *en famille*. In fact, Gregory was not only a beleaguered bishop, but originally a reluctant one too. He had remained unbaptised for many years and was prompted to make a public profession of Christianity at least partly because of a terrifying dream in which the martyrs appeared to him and reproached and beat him for his indifference. Thus, he became a reader in the church, but his love of rhetoric soon made him give this up for the profession of rhetorician. There is good, but much disputed, evidence to suggest that he married a certain Theosebeia at this time, who until her death remained his wife even after he became bishop, a practice definitively repudiated only later in the time of Justinian (527–565).[7] However this may be, it was through Macrina that Gregory finally withdrew from the world to live a life of prayer and study at his brother's monastery, from which he was summoned, against his vigorous protest, by Basil to take up the bishopric of Nyssa in about 370. Undoubtedly, Gregory was a gentle, retiring spirit who preferred study and reflection to the life of action, perhaps a little simple and naive in the labyrinth of public affairs. At any rate, charges of embezzlement of church funds were brought against him by the Arian faction and in 376 he was banished to Seleucia by the emperor, Valens. All of the torment of this experience Gregory relates to his sister and the reply Gregory puts into her mouth is not without a wry humour directed against himself. She upbraids him:

> Will you not put an end to your failure to recognise the good things which come from God? . . . Churches send you forth and call upon you as ally and reformer, and you do not see the grace in this? Do you not even realise the true cause of such great blessings, that our parents' prayers are lifting you on high, for you have little or no native capacity for this?

This is part of the great charm of the VSM, that it reveals to us, however unconsciously, the gentle, saintly character of the famous, beleaguered bishop who acknowledges with a faint smile the justice of his elder sister's reproach. In the VSM the people of the fourth century come alive, passionate and with humour even at the most sacred moments. Witness the account of Macrina's healing of a little girl's eye disease towards the end of the story. The soldier and his wife return so enchanted from their visit to the monastery that they have utterly forgotten Macrina's promised cure, and even the little girl herself, it seems:

> And I recounted all I had seen and heard in the men's enclosure, while she told me every little thing in detail, like a history book, and thought that she should omit nothing, not even the least significant details. On she went, telling about everything . . . as if in a narrative, and when she came to the part where a promise of a cure for the eye had been made, she interrupted the narrative to exclaim, "What's the matter with us? How did we forget?"

Unforgettable too is a final, vivid glimpse which Gregory gives us of his sister, from the same story about the miracle and after the account of her death and burial. To the soldier, as to everyone else, she is "the great Macrina," "the holy one," but the picture Gregory infuses into his words is of a young girl, thoroughly alive, with an almost mischievous twinkle in her eye:

> [the blessed Macrina] . . . held our little daughter in her arms and said that she would not give her back until she had given them a meal. . . . "If you do me the favour of sharing our table with us, I will give you in return a reward to match your courtesy."

What could be more natural or more feminine than this? Thus, we can see that, as in Dostoevski's portrait of Fr. Zossima in *The Brothers Karamazov,* the holy one is not she who is most remote from life, but she who was always at the heart of it.

TRADITIONAL TYPOLOGY FOR MACRINA

& THE IDEAL OF PHILOSOPHY

Gregory wrote two works about Macrina (together referred to as *Ta Makrinia*, "The Macrina Works"), the VSM and a dialogue on the soul and the resurrection, the *De Anima et Resurrectione*. The two works are independent, but they refer to one another and should be read together, since the dialogue is in fact the long conversation Macrina had with Gregory upon his arrival at the monastery. Behind the personal tribute in these works there lies a deeper typology at work: Macrina is the virgin-philosopher par excellence, and although Gregory wants us to see the type, or deeper imprint of tradition in her, the type which Macrina embodies is nonetheless unique. In the VSM Macrina is presented as a second Thekla, the legendary virgin[8] who, in the apocryphal *Acts of Paul and Thekla*, is the faithful disciple to whom St. Paul entrusts the continuation of his apostolic ministry. This traditional continuity Gregory intimates not only in the dream which his mother Emmelia has when she is in labour with Macrina, but in his insistence that Macrina is a teacher, a leader and a mistress of Scripture. Her incomparably beautiful deathbed prayer bears witness to the fact that Holy Scripture permeated her every word. In the dialogue (so reminiscent of Socrates' death bed scene and his arguments for the immortality of the soul in the *Phaedo*), Macrina is presented as the Christian Socrates, equal to, or even surpassing, that profound intelligence. The Socratic typology also enters into the VSM, both in the "ideal of philosophy" which is central to Macrina's life and also in the dramatic fibre of the whole work, centred upon the death bed of a mighty religious and intellectual leader. The idea of putting the two figures, Thekla and Socrates, together might have been suggested to Gregory by a work written in the second half of the third century, the *Symposion* of Methodius of Olympus (after Plato's famous Socratic dialogue of the same name) in which a group of ten women, whose intellectual leader is Thekla, discuss the theme of virginity at a banquet, instead of love (ἔρος) as in Plato's *Symposium*. In the VSM and the dialogue, however, Gregory weaves these two themes together in such a natural way within the figure of Macrina that there is nothing procrustean or out of place about the union. Furthermore, the ideal of philosophy itself is so central to Macrina's monastic life that we undoubtedly hear the original phrases when the soldier tells of St. Peter's pressing invitation to take part in "the philosophic table." The question arises therefore: Could Macrina really have been such an intellectual figure? Is this not merely Gregory's own art contriving to hand down a tradition, the tradition of apostolic women? And there is something even more pressing than this: Gregory himself tells us in the VSM that Macrina was educated primarily in the Scriptures and certainly not in the great models of profane culture, the pagan poets. How then could the real Macrina in the dialogue on the soul have spoken with consummate ease upon philosophical topics and with detailed knowledge of pagan philosophy, especially Stoic and Epicurean thought?

It is evident that we can not ultimately determine what belongs to Macrina herself and what to Gregory. But in this case, I would suggest, the fact was probably more arresting, and indeed unique, than any fiction could ever have been. In our own times we are more fortunate than in some past eras and much more aware that we can learn real and important things, even academic things, without ever having stepped inside the classroom. We have tended, it is true, to think of education in antiquity after the fashion of our own image and to imagine even "Faculties of administration" when we heard of the great "schools" of Alexandria and Athens. But we also know that the likes of Origen and Plotinus certainly did not learn their philosophy in such places but, instead, at the feet of an almost anonymous master, Ammonius Sacchas, outside his hut in some remote location which must have seemed the very end of the earth. Now Macrina was evidently a genius. She was also the sister, mother, teacher and spiritual guide in a family of distinguished advocates, philosophers, theologians and bishops. Everything points, therefore, to the simplest and most obvious interpretation that she was an intellectual and religious focus for a growing family. And indeed we may also observe that the unification of the Thekla-Socrates figures in Macrina was probably made possible for Gregory by the fact that the Macrina he knew and loved was the Macrina he had always gone to for advice and spiritual guidance and really was the Macrina with whom he had always debated his most pressing philosophical and theological problems. Whether Macrina had had formal philosophical training or not, she was at the centre of an intellectual family. I suggest, therefore, that we possess an excellent example in Macrina of the breadth of informal education in the great homes of the fourth century.

Finally, the ideal of philosophy in the VSM is in stark contrast to the sometimes narrow, academic discipline we know today. Its roots for Gregory lie in a living tradition which includes and, for the Christian, perfects the best of pagan thought, especially that of Socrates and Plato. For Macrina and Gregory philosophy is the spirit of living wisdom which embraces the whole of human life: prayer, manual work, hospitality, care of the sick, of the poor and the dying. It is a life entirely given to God, a life not without risk, a life lived "on the boundaries" of human nature. It includes a vibrant intellectuality, life-long study and a spirit of true inquiry, and it culminates in the divine love of a person, Christ. This life is the reversal of our normal, material perceptions ("not to be known was their fame, their wealth was in possessing nothing," and one can also see in the VSM implicit indications of how it surpasses the philosophic ideals of the pagans.

First of all, Gregory acutely perceives that the *Phaedo,* Plato's dialogue about the immortality of the soul, set on the day of Socrates' death, is not just a series of arguments but the dramatic situation of the hero before death, and therefore the deeper reality of every human situation in life lifted to a new intensity. The *Phaedo* ends with Socrates' death and we, the audience, are implicitly challenged by the spiritual reality of the soul which Socrates has presented, and also by that of his own life, to make a choice between lives: the life of the spirit or that of the body. Our own faith or the lack of it is also what concerns Gregory at the end of the VSM . We are left to decide for ourselves what choice we will make.

However, the differences between the *Phaedo* and the VSM (and the dialogue on the soul) are also instructive. The *Phaedo* focuses attention upon the living reality which is the soul, the VSM also includes the body. The *Phaedo* concludes with Socrates' gradual death from the hemlock; and the body is wrapped entirely in its cloak, for Socrates at least, a thing no longer of any consequence. The VSM, however, takes us through the death and beyond, the body is laid out before our eyes and is still beautiful, it is buried and Gregory's repugnance to look upon the decomposed bodies of his parents leaves us with no illusions as to its mortal fate; but we are left nonetheless with the picture of the living Macrina in the story of the miracles described above. In the *Phaedo* it is the men alone who discuss the weighty matter of life and death; Xanthippe and the women are excluded. In the VSM it is a woman among women who is the centre of attention.

There are many insights to be drawn from these differences, and among them are the following.

Firstly, in the Christian perspective both soul and body make up the whole God-created person. Therefore, even though the soul is of greater value, made in God's image and an immaterial reality, the life of the body is also crucial for salvation.

Secondly, the Christian is concerned not so much with the finality of death as with the natural transition into new life. The focus, then, is not upon one's own soul, but upon the goodness of God's grace, love and mercy towards us by which he grants increase to all human efforts.

Thirdly, man and woman are fully equal, since in Christ there is neither male nor female, but in him all are one. For Gregory distinctions of sex are irrelevant to the life one lives in God and will in fact disappear in heaven. It is ironic, however, that this fundamental equality should be so poignantly demonstrated by a woman who is clearly superior to everyone else and who remains decidedly feminine even up to the end.

And finally, the goal (σκοπός) of philosophy is the natural, unceasing progression of the whole self into true loving union with God. In this natural, organic progression are united the frequent (Pauline) images of the athlete's unceasing struggle to win the race, to fight the good fight, and the more comprehensive monastic ideal of living wisdom. For true philosophy, then, death is not the end of discovery, but the culminating moment in the Christian's giving up of herself to others and to God, which is in turn the discovery of all that God has given her to be.

TEXTS, TRANSLATIONS,

& ABBREVIATIONS

The text used throughout is *Gregorii Nysseni Opera Ascetica* (GN 8/ 1), ed. W. Jaeger, J.-P. Cavarnos, V. Woods Callahan (Leiden, 1952). In this edition, the VSM was edited by Virginia Woods Callahan (pp. 347–414). Occasionally I have followed P. Maraval's text where this was clearly superior: *Grégoire de Nysse: Vie de Saint Macrine,* introd., texte critique, trad., notes et index par P. Maraval, Sources Chrétiennes (Paris: Cerf, 1971).

Two translations have been consulted: the excellent English translation by V. Woods Callahan in *Saint Gregory of Nyssa: Ascetical Works,* The Fathers of the Church series 58 (Washington, 1967) and the French translation by P. Maraval, cited above, with most helpful notes.

FROM GREGORY,

BISHOP OF NYSSA,

A LETTER ON

THE LIFE OF SAINT MACRINA

This is work appears from the general form of the heading, to be a letter, but it exceeds the limits of a letter and stretches into a lengthy narrative. My excuse, however, is that the subject you ordered me to write upon is too big to be treated within the proper bounds of a letter.

You certainly cannot have forgotten our meeting when, on my way to visit Jerusalem in order to fulfill a vow[9] to see the signs of the Lord's residence in the flesh in those places, I ran into you in the city of Antioch and we discussed all sorts of things (for it was hardly likely to be a silent meeting with your keen intelligence prompting numerous starting-points for discussion); and, as often happens in these cases, in the course of our conversation we recalled the life of an honoured person; it was a woman who prompted our narrative, if, that is, we may call her a woman, for I do not know if it is appropriate to apply a name drawn from nature to one who has risen above nature.

Our narrative was not based on hearsay, but we talked with detailed knowledge of things our own experience has taught us, without appealing to any outside testimony; for the maiden we spoke of was no stranger to my family so that I had to learn from others the marvels of her life. No, we had the same parents and she was, so to speak, a votive offering of the fruits to come, the first offshoot of our mother's womb.

And so, since you were convinced that the story of her good deeds would be of some use because you thought that a life of this quality should not be forgotten for the future and that she who had raised herself through philosophy[10] to the highest limit of human virtue should not pass along this way veiled and in silence, I thought it good to obey you and tell her story, as briefly as I could, in a simple, unaffected narrative.

The maiden was called Macrina. Some time ago, there had been a celebrated Macrina in our family, our father's mother. At the time of the persecutions she had suffered bravely for her confession of faith in Christ,[11] and it was in honour of her that the child was given this name by her parents. But this was her public name used by her acquaintances; another name had been secretly given her as the result of a vision which had occurred during labour before she emerged into the light of day. For, in fact, her mother was so virtuous a person that she let herself be led by the will of God in everything and had embraced an exceptionally pure and spotless way of life with the result that she had even chosen of her own free will not to marry. But since she was bereft of both parents,[12] and because her body was just springing into full bud[13] and the fame of her fairness had drawn many young men together in pursuit of her hand, there was a risk that if she were not by her own choice united with someone, she might against her will suffer some violence because the suitors were maddened by her beauty and were getting ready to carry her off. For this reason she chose a man known and proven for the uprightness of his life so that she acquired a guardian for her own life. In her very first pregnancy she became the mother of Macrina.

And when the time came when she was to be freed from her labour pain by giving birth to the child, she fell asleep and seemed to be carrying in her arms the child still embraced by her womb, and someone in suprahuman majesty of form and shape appeared to address the little child by the name of Thekla, that Thekla of great fame among maidens.[14] After doing this three times and calling upon her to witness it,[15] the person disappeared from her sight and gave ease to her labour pains so that as soon as she woke up from her sleep she saw that the dream was reality. And so that was Macrina's secret name. In my view, however, the figure who appeared declared this not so much to guide the mother in her choice of name as to foretell the life of the child and to point out, by the identity of name, a similarity in their choice of life.

And so the child grew. Although she also had her own nurse, for the most part her mother nursed her herself. When she had passed the age of infancy, she was quick to learn her children's lessons, and whatever lessons her parents decided to have the girl study, in those the nature of the little girl excelled.

It was a matter of serious interest to her mother to instruct the child, but not in this pagan, secular course of where the students' early years are for the most part formed by the study of the poets.[16] For she held that it was shameful and altogether unfitting to teach a tender and easily influenced nature either the passions of tragedy – those passions of women[17] which have given the poets their sources of inspiration and their plots – or the indecent revels of comedy, or the causes of the evils which befell Troy,[18] definitely spoiling the child's nature with the really rather irreverent tales about women. Instead, any passages of divinely inspired Scripture which seemed accessible to very young persons, were the child's study, and above all, the Wisdom of Solomon, and after this,[19] whatever was conducive to the moral life.[20] But also there was none of the psalms which she did not know since she recited each part of the Psalter at the proper times of the day, when she rose from her bed, performed or rested from her duties, sat down to eat or rose up from the table, when she went to bed or got up to pray, at all time she had the Psalter with her like a good travelling companion who never fails.[21]

Growing up with these and similar occupations and having become especially skilled in the working of wool, she attained her twelfth year, the age in which the bloom of youth starts to radiate more that at any other time.

Here it is indeed worth marvelling how the beauty of the young girl, although concealed, did not remain unnoticed. There did not seem to be any such marvel in the whole of that country which could compare with her beauty and gracefulness, so that not even painters' hands could come close to her fresh beauty; and the art which engineers everything and which dares even to wrestle with the greatest subjects, going so far as to fashion in imitation images of the planets themselves,[22] did not have the power to render a true likeness of her blessed beauty. Because of this, a great swarm of suitors surrounded her parents. But her father (for he was indeed wise and practised in the discernment of what is noble) chose from the rest of the company a young kinsman of good repute, known for the moderation of his life who had recently finished school and decided to betroth his daughter to him when she came of age. Meanwhile the young man was among his brighter hopes and brought to the girl's father his reputation for oratory, like a pleasing wedding gift, demonstrating his rhetorical ability in lawsuits on behalf of people who had been wronged. But Envy[23] cut short the bright promise by plucking him from life at a pitiable early age.

The young girl was not unaware of her father's resolution, but when the young man's death had broken off what had been decided for her, she called her father's decision a marriage, as if what had been decided upon had in fact really happened, and she determined to remain by herself for the rest of her life, a decision which was more firmly rooted than one might have expected in one of her age.

Her parents brought up the subject of marriage to her on many occasions because of the many young men who as a result of her famed beauty, wanted to sue for her hand, but she would say that is was improper, indeed unlawful, for her not to embrace a marriage which had been concluded for her once and for all by her father and to be forced instead to look to another when marriage, like birth and death, is by nature something that only happens once. She strongly insisted that the young man who had been joined to her in accordance with her parents' decision was not dead, but that, in her judgement, he who was living in God because of the hope of the resurrection,[24] was simply away from home on a journey and not a dead body; and it was improper not to keep faith with a husband who was away on a journey.

By arguments such as these she pushed aside those who were trying to persuade her and she hit upon one safeguard for her good decision, never to be separated from her mother even for a moment, so that her mother often said to her that she had been pregnant with the rest of her children for the prescribed term, but as for Macrina she bore her always and everywhere, embracing her, as it were, in her womb. But sharing her life with her daughter was not hard for the mother nor was it without benefit. For, instead of her many maidservants, there was now the attentive care of her daughter and a true exchange was realised between the two of them. The older woman cared for the young girl's soul, the young girl for her mother's bodily needs, fulfilling in all things[25] the service that was needed, even frequently preparing bread with her own hands for her mother. This was not her first preoccupation, but after she had lent[26] her hands in service to the liturgies, she thought this occupation fitting for her way of life and, in the time she had left, she provided food for her mother by her own toil; and not only this, but she also took an active part helping her mother in all her pressing concerns; for her mother had four sons and five daughters and was paying taxes to three governors, since her property was scattered throughout that number of provinces.[27]

In many different ways, then, her mother was divided by the worries of this situation – for Macrina's father had already departed this life – and Macrina was a partner to her in all these tasks, taking an equal share in her worries and alleviating the burden of her sufferings. Furthermore, under the guidance of her mother, she kept her own life spotless, being directed in everything by the approval of her mother's eyes; and at the same time by the example of her own life she provided great guidance to her mother towards the same goal, namely that of philosophy, drawing her on little by little to the immaterial,[28] more perfect life.

And when her mother had arranged in a fair and fitting way the situations of her sisters with a view to what seemed best for each of them, the great Basil, brother of the girl we have been speaking about, came back from the school where he had been trained for a long time in the discipline of rhetoric. Although when she took him in hand he was monstrously conceited about his skill in rhetoric, contemptuous of every high reputation and exalted beyond the leading lights of the province by his self-importance, so swiftly did she win him to the ideal of philosophy that he renounced worldly appearance, showed contempt for the admiration of rhetorical ability and went over of his own accord to this active life of manual labour, preparing for himself by means of his complete poverty a way of life which would tend without impediment towards virtue. But the life of Basil and the subsequent activities for which he became famous in every land under the sun and, by his reputation, eclipsed all those who were illustrious for virtue, would need a lengthy narrative and a lot of time to tell; so then let my story be turned back again to the subject before it.

Since any reason for living a more materialistic way of life was now taken away, Macrina persuaded her mother to give up their accustomed way of life, their rather ostentatious life-style and the services she had previously been accustomed to receive from her maids, and she also persuaded her to put herself on an equal footing with the many in spirit and to share a common life with all her maids, making them sisters and equals instead of slaves and servants. But I would prefer here to make a small insertion into my narrative and not to leave unrecorded an event so noteworthy as to bear further witness to the sublime character of the maiden.

The second of her four brothers after the great Basil was called Naucratius, and he surpassed the others in the good fortune of his nature, his physical beauty, strength, swiftness and facility for everything. At the age of twenty-one he gave such proofs of his industry at a public recital that the whole assembled audience was deeply moved by him, but prompted by some divine providence he looked down upon all the opportunities at hand and went off in some real inspiration of thought to a life of solitude and poverty, taking nothing with him but himself. One of his servants, however, Chysaphios, followed him, both because of his friendship for him and because he was intent upon the same choice of life.

So he lived by himself, settled in a remote spot by the Iris. The Iris is a river which flows through the middle of the province of Pontus, has its source in Armenia and empties itself by way of our own lands into the Black Sea. Close by this river the young man found a spot thickly covered by deep forest, hidden in a hollow of an overhanging mountain range, and there he lived far from the disturbances of the city and from the preoccupations of military service or of the rhetoric of the law courts. And having freed himself from all the usual, resounding noise of human life, with his own hands he took care of a group of old people living together in poverty and sickness, since he considered it fitting to make this type of service the care of his personal life. Because he was skilled in every sort of hunting technique, he would go hunting to provide food for the old people and at the same time to disciplining his youthful vigour by such tasks; but he also eagerly complied with his mother's wishes, if she ever asked something of him, and in both of these ways he kept his life upright and true, controlling his youthful vigour both by his labours and by obedient attention to his mother; and through observance of the divine commandments he made his way to God.

For five years he lived in this way, dedicating himself to philosophy and making his mother's life truly happy both because he ordered his own life with moderation and because he put all his strength into obeying the wishes of her who had given him birth. Then, a grievous, tragic accident happened for the mother; it was planned, I think, by the Adversary, and was enough to bring our whole family to misfortune and sorrow. All of a sudden he was snatched from life, and it was not sickness which prepares one to anticipate death nor any other of the usual recognisable causes which brought death to the young man.

He had gone out to hunt, his means of procuring the necessaries of life for the old people in his care, but his dead body was brought back home – both he and Chrysaphios, his companion. His mother was far away from what was taking place, three days' journey from the disaster, and someone came to tell her what had happened. Perfect though she was in every kind of virtue, nature prevailed all the same even over her. She became breathless and speechless and fainted away on the spot, reason giving way to grievous shock, and she lay under the assault of the dreadful news like an athlete of noble stock felled by an unexpected blow.

In this tragedy the excellence of the great Macrina became clear. Placing reason in opposition to passion, she kept herself from falling and, by becoming a support to her mother's weakness, she drew her back again from the depths of her grief. With her firm, unflinching spirit she taught her mother's soul to be brave.

⌈Consequently, her mother was not swept away by her sorrow, nor did she give vent to her suffering in any base or womanish way[29]⌉

so as to shout out against her evil fortune, tear her cloak, bewail her suffering or stir up lamentations and their mournful chantings. Instead she endured the attacks of nature with calm, resisting them with her own reasoned reflections and with those suggested by her daughter in order to heal her pain. For then above all, the sublime and exalted soul of the young girl made itself manifest, because her nature also experienced its own suffering; for it was her brother and her most beloved brother, who had been snatched away by death in such a way. Nevertheless, she rose above nature and by means of her own reasoned reflections[30] she lifted her mother up together with her and placed her beyond suffering, guiding her to patience and courage by her own example. But, most of all, her life offered her mother no opportunity to give vent to sorrow at the thought of him who was absent, and instead gave her occasion to delight in the good which she could see before her.

When the responsibility of bringing up the children and the worry of their education and establishment in life was over, and when most of the resources for the more material side of life were shared out among the children, then, as mentioned before, the life of the maiden became for her mother a guide towards the philosophical, immaterial way of life. Turning her away from all she was accustomed to, she led her to her own standard of humility, prepared her to put herself on an equal footing with the community of maidens, so as to share on equal terms with them one table, bed and all the needs of life, with every difference of rank eliminated from their lives.

And such was the order of their life, such was the high level of philosophy and the holy conduct of their living by day and by night that it exceeds the power of words to describe it. For just as souls are freed from their bodies by death and at the same time liberated from the cares of this life, so was their existence separated from these things, removed from all of life's vanity and fashioned in harmonious imitation of the life of the angels. In them no anger, envy, hate, arrogance, nor any other such thing was seen; the desire for foolish things of no substance, for honour, glory, delusions of grandeur, the need to be superior to others, and all such things had been eradicated. Self-control was their pleasure, not to be known was their fame, their wealth was in possessing nothing and in shaking off[31] all material surplus, like dust from the body; their work was none of the concerns of this life, except in so far as it was a subordinate task.[32] Their only care was for divine realities, and there was constant prayer[33] and the unceasing singing of hymns, extended equally throughout the entire day and night so that this was both work and respite from work for them.

What human works could ever bring such a mode of existence before one's gaze – in a community whose way of life lay at the boundaries[34] between human nature and the nature which is without body? For to have freed nature from human passions was a feat beyond human strength, while to appear in body, to be encompassed by bodily shape and to live with the organs of sense was thereby to possess a nature inferior to that of the angelic and the incorporeal. Perhaps one might even go so far as to say that the difference was minimal, because, although they lived in the flesh, by virtue of their affinity with the incorporeal powers they were not weighed down by the attractive pull of the body, but their lives were borne upwards, poised on high and they took their souls' flight[35] in concert with the heavenly powers. The time spent in such a way of life was not short and their accomplishments increased with time, since philosophy always granted them an abundance of help in the discovery of good things which led them on to greater purity.[36]

Macrina had a brother who was of special assistance towards this great goal of life. His name was Peter, and with him our mother's birth pangs ceased; for he was the last, tender shoot of his parents, called both son and orphan because at the moment he came into the light of this life, his father departed from it. However, right at the time of his birth when he had only been a few moments at the breast, his eldest sister, the subject of our story, snatched him straight up from the woman who was nursing him and brought him up herself, and she led him to all the higher learning, exercising him from infancy in the sacred teachings so as not to give his soul the leisure to incline to any profane pursuit.

She became everything for the child, father teacher, guide, mother, counsellor in every good, and she perfected him in such a way that before he left childhood, while he was still blossoming at the tender stage of adolescent youth, he was lifted up towards the sublime goal of philosophy; and by some happy, natural disposition he possessed a skillfulness for every kind of handicraft so that without having had anyone to teach him the art in all its specific details, he succeeded in mastering skills for which the majority of people require a long and laborious apprenticeship. He looked down, then, on the practice of profane studies, and holding nature as a sufficient teacher of all good learning and always looking to his sister and making her the ideal of every good, he made such progress in virtue that he was of no less repute than the great Basil for the superior qualities of his later life. But then, in preference to everything, he was working together with his sister and mother with a view to that angelic life. Once, when there was a severe famine and many people from all over, drawn by the fame of their generosity, came pouring into the remote country in which they lived, he provided such an abundance of provisions, thanks to his inventiveness,[37] that because of the throng of visitors, the wilderness looked like a city.

Meanwhile, our mother, who had reached a rich old age,

migrated to God; and it was in the arms of both of her children that she left her earthly life. It is worth recording the blessing she pronounced upon her children; she remembered, as was fitting, each of those not present so that no one of them should be without a share of her blessing, and she especially entrusted those present to God in her prayer. These two of her children sat on either side of her bed, she took hold of the hand of each and addressed these, her last words, to God:

> To you, O Lord, do I offer the first and the tenth fruit
> of my labour pains. This is my first born, my eldest
> daughter, and this my tenth child, my last born son. To
> you, both have been consecrated by law and your votive
> offerings they are. So may sanctification come to this my
> first and to this my tenth born.

And her words clearly betokened her daughter and son. When she had finished her blessing, she ended her life, having instructed her children to place her body in our father's tomb.

They fulfilled her command and devoted themselves in a still more sublime fashion to philosophy, always carrying on the struggle with their own lives and overshadowing their earlier accomplishments with those that followed.

Meanwhile, Basil, a man distinguished among holy people, was chosen to be bishop of the great church of Caesarea and he led his brother to the vocation of the priesthood in the council of elders, ordaining them in the sacred rites himself. By this too their lives made progress in piety and holiness because the priesthood gave increase to their philosophy. Eight years after this, Basil, famed throughout the whole world, departed the life of men and went to God,[38] and his death was a common source of sorrow for both his own country and the world.

When Macrina in her retreat far away heard the news of his

death, her soul was deeply upset at such a great loss (for how could suffering fail to touch her too, when even the enemies of the truth were affected?). But just as they say the quality of gold is purified in different melting-pots, that if anything escapes the first casting, it is separated out in the second, and again in the final casting all impurity mixed in with the metal is cleansed from it, and the most accurate test of true gold is if, having come through the whole casting process, it gives off no further impurity;[39] something similar to this happened also in Macrina's case.

The high quality of her thinking was thoroughly tested by successive attacks of painful grief to reveal the authentic and undebased nature of her soul, first by the death of her other brother, Naucratios, after this by the separation from her mother and third when Basil, the common honour of our family, departed from human life. So she stood her ground like an undefeated athlete, who does not cringe at any point before the onslaught of misfortune.

Nine months, or a little more, after this a synod of bishops was convened in the city of Antioch, in which I also took part. And when we were free to return again, each to his own diocese, before the year went by it was weighing heavy on my heart, I, Gregory, to go and visit her. For it was a long time since our last meeting during which the critical circumstances of my trials had prevented our visiting each other, since I was constantly being exiled by the leaders of heresy.[40] And when I counted up the intervening time in which my trials had precluded our seeing each other, no brief interval did it appear – it came to almost eight years. And so when I had finished most of the journey and was only one day's travel away from her, I had a vision in a dream which made me apprehensive for the future. I seemed to be holding in my hands the relics of martyrs, and there came from them a bright gleam of light, as from a flawless mirror which had been placed face to the sun, so that my eyes were blinded by the brilliance of the gleam.

During that same night this vision occurred three times, and I was not able to interpret clearly the dreams' hidden meaning, but I foresaw some distress for my soul and I awaited the outcome to make a judgment about what had appeared to me. And in fact when I did get close to the remote spot in which she spent her angelic, heavenly life, I asked one of her community first if my brother was there. He told me that he had set out about three days ago to meet me, and I understood what had happened, that he had taken another road to meet us. Then I enquired of the great Macrina; and when he told me that she was sick, I was in an even greater hurry to finish the rest of the journey, for in truth a foreboding of what was to happen had come upon me and was troubling me deeply.

As I was arriving at the place itself (and the news of my presence had already been announced to the community), an entire contingent of men poured forth from the monastic enclosure – for it was customary for them to honour guests by coming out to greet them – and a group of maidens from the convent awaited our coming by the church in good order.[41]

When the prayers and blessing had been completed and the women had bowed their hands respectfully to receive the blessing and had retired to their own quarters, since none of them remained behind with me, I guessed correctly that their Superior[42] was not among them. Someone guided me to the house where the great Macrina was, opened the door, and there I was inside that holy place. Macrina was already caught in the grip of a grievous sickness, but she was resting not on a bed or a couch, but on the ground, on a plank covered with sack-cloth, with another plank supporting her head and designed to serve instead of a pillow, lying under her neck muscles at a raised angle and giving the right amount of support to her neck.

When she saw me standing by the door, she raised herself on her elbow, but she was unable to run up to me because her strength had already been undermined by the fever. But, planting her hands on the bare floor and stretching forward as far as she could reach from her bed, she managed to do me the honour of greeting me; and I ran up to her, and taking her bowed head in my hands, I lifted her up and put her back in her accustomed reclining position. And she stretched out her hand to God and said, "Even this favour you have fulfilled for me, my God, and you have not deprived me of my heart's desire in that you have inspired your servant to visit your handmaiden." And so that she might not bring any despondency to my soul, she tried to stifle her groans and forced herself somehow to hide her tortured gasping for breath.

Throughout everything she was trying to create a more cheerful mood, and she initiated suitable topics of conversation and gave me the opportunity to speak by the questions she asked. But when in the course of our conversation we inadvertently made mention of the great Basil, then my heart sank, my face fell in sorrow and the tears poured from my eyes. But she was so far from being downcast by our sorrow that she made our mention of the holy man a starting point for the higher philosophy, and she expounded arguments of such excellence, explaining the human situation in terms of natural causes, unveiling to reason the divine providence hidden in sad events and recounting in detail events of the life to be hereafter as if she were inspired by the Holy Spirit, that my soul seemed to be almost outside of human nature, uplifted as it was by her words and set down inside the heavenly sanctuaries by the guidance of her discourse.[43]

And just as we hear in the story of Job, that the man was wasting away covered at every point of his entire body with festering and oozing sores, and yet he did not allow his perception, by means of his power of reasoned reflection, to incline towards his pain, but kept the faculty which felt the pain in the body, and would neither blunt the edge of his concentration upon his own proper activity nor interrupt the conversation when it embarked on high matters;[44] it was something like this that I was also seeing in the case of the great Macrina; although the fever was devouring all her strength and driving her headlong to death, she refreshed her body as if with some kind of morning dew, and so she kept her mind unhindered in the contemplation of sublime things, without being at all affected by a sickness of such severity.

And were it not that my narrative was stretching out to infinity, I would record everything in the order and way it happened: how she was lifted up by her discourse and spoke to me of her philosophy of the soul; how she explained the reason for life in the flesh, for what purpose man exists, how he is mortal, what is the source of death and what release there is from death back to life again. On all of these subjects, as if inspired by the power of the Holy Spirit, she explained everything clearly and logically, her speech flowing on with complete ease as water is borne from some fountain-head downhill without anything to get in its way.

When our conversation was concluded, she said, "It's time, brother, for you to rest your body for a little while, as your journey must have tired you out," while for me it was really a complete relaxation just to look at her and to listen to her noble words; but since this was pleasing and important to her, in order that I might show obedience to my teacher in everything, I found ready for me in one of the nearby gardens a beautiful spot to rest in and I took my repose under the shade of the vine-girt trees.

It was, however, not possible to savour the delightful surroundings when my soul within was awash with foreboding of unhappy events; for what I had seen seemed to unveil the hidden meaning of the vision in my dream. What I had seen before me was truly the remains of a holy martyr, one who had been dead to sin,[45] but illumined by the indwelling grace of the Holy Spirit.[46] And I explained this to one of those who had already heard my account of the Dream.

We were in the depths of despondency (as was only natural) in the anticipation of sad events, but Macrina guessed (I know not how) our state of mind and sent a message of better tidings to us, telling us to cheer up and to be of better hopes for her; for she perceived a turn for the better. This was not said to deceive us, but her communication was absolutely truthful, even if we did not recognise it at the time. For, in reality, just as a runner who has overtaken his rival and is already close to the finish of the race-course, when he draws near to the prize and sees the victor's crown, rejoices in his heart, as though he had already won the prizes which lie before him, and proclaims his victory to his supporters in the audience, from a similar intention Macrina gave us to hope for greater things for her, since she was already looking towards the prize of her upward calling[47] and all but applying the words of the apostle to herself when he says that "all there is to come now is the crown of righteousness reserved for me, which the righteous judge will give to me,"[48] since "I have fought the good fight, I have run the race to the end and I have kept the faith."[49] Reassured, then, by this good news, we started to enjoy the things that were put before us, and these were varied, the provision full of intent to give pleasure, since the great Macrina's thoughtfulness extended even to these things.

When we were again in her presence – for she did not allow us to spend much time on our own – she took up the story of the events of her life from infancy and retold them all in order as in an historical narrative, what she could remember about our parents' life, what happened before my birth and what afterwards.

The aim of her story was to give thanks to God. For, as regards the life of our parents, she emphasised not so much their brilliant prosperity at the time and the fact that they were admired everywhere, as that they had been given increase in abundance by God's love for mankind.[50] Our father's parents had their possessions confiscated for their profession of Christ. Our mother's grandfather had been put to death because he had angered the emperor and all his belongings passed to other masters. And in spite of this, their livelihood increased to such an extent because of their faith that there was no one more reputed than they were among the people of that time. Again, when their wealth was divided in nine ways according to the number of their children, the portion given to each was so multiplied by divine blessing that each child lived more prosperously than the parents had done. And of the wealth singled out for her in the equal distribution among the brothers and sisters, Macrina herself retained nothing, but everything was given into the hands of the priest to be administered in accordance with the divine commandment.[51]

Her life was such, since God provided for her, that she never stopped working her hands in the service of God[52] nor did she ever look to man for help nor through any human agency did there come to her the opportunity for a life of comfort. But neither did she turn away people who sought her help nor did she seek out benefactors, for God with His blessings secretly made the small resources from her good works grow like seeds into an abundant stream of fruitfulness.

I then told her all about the personal troubles I had, earlier when the emperor, Valens, had driven me into exile for the faith and later when confusion reigned in the churches and drew me into disputes and wearisome effort.

"Will you not put an end," she asked "to your failure to recognise the good things which come from God? Will you not compare your lot with that of your parents? And yet it is true that according to the standard of this world we can have great pride most of all in this that we were well born and from noble stock.

"Our father was very well thought of in his day for his education," she continued, "but his reputation only extended to the law-courts of his own land. Later on, although he was a long way ahead of everybody else in his mastery of rhetoric, his fame did not reach outside Pontus, but he was glad to be widely recognised in his own country. But you," she said, "are known in the cities, the townships and the provinces. Churches send you forth and call upon you as ally and reformer, and you do not see the grace in this? Do you not even realise the true cause of such great blessings, that our parents' prayers are lifting you on high, for you have little or no native capacity for this?"

While she was saying this, I kept wishing that the day could be lengthened so that she might not cease to delight our hearing; but the singing of the choir was calling us to the evening thanksgiving prayers, and the great Macrina sent me off to church too and withdrew herself to God in prayer. And the night was spent in these devotions.

When day came, it was clear to me from what I saw that this day was to mark her last in the life of the flesh, since the fever had totally spent all her natural, inbuilt strength. She saw our dispirited thinking and tried to bring us out of our despondency by again dispersing the pain of our souls with those beautiful words of hers, but from now on her breathing was shallow and tortured.

It was at this moment above all that my soul was torn by what confronted it; on the one hand, my nature was heavy with sadness, as is understandable, in the anticipation that I would no longer hear that voice of hers; but, on the other hand, in so far as I did not yet grasp that the glory of our whole family was going to leave this human life, my soul was divinely inspired, as it were, by the things I saw and I suspected that she had transcended the common nature. For not even in her last breaths to feel anything strange in the expectation of death nor to fear separation from life, but with sublime thinking to philosophise upon what she had chosen for this life,[53] right from the beginning up to her last breath, to me this seemed no longer to be a part of human realities. Instead, it was as if an angel had providentially assumed human form, an angel in whom there was no affinity for, nor attachment to, the life of the flesh, about whom it was not unreasonable that her thinking should remain impassible,[54] since the flesh did not drag it down to its own passions. For this reason she seemed to me to be making manifest to those then present that pure, divine love of the unseen bridegroom, which she had nourished secretly in the most intimate depths of her soul, and she seemed to transmit the desire which was in her heart to rush to the one she longed for, so that freed from the fetters of the body, she might swiftly be with him. For it was really towards her beloved that she ran, and no other of life's pleasures ever turned her eye to itself away from her beloved.

Most of the day had already passed and the sun was starting to set. Her fervour, however, did not give way, but the more she neared her departure, the more she contemplated the beauty of the bridegroom and longed to rush impulsively to her beloved. She no longer spoke to us who were present, but to that one alone upon whom she held her eyes intently. Her bed had been turned towards the east, and she stopped conversing with us and was with God in prayer for the rest of the time, reaching out her hands in supplication and speaking in a low, faint voice so that we could only just hear

what she said. This was her prayer and there is no doubt that it
to God and was heard by him.

She said:

You have released us, O Lord, from the fear of death.[55]
You have made the end of life here on earth
a beginning of true life for us.
You let our bodies rest in sleep in due season
and you awaken them again
at the soundof the last trumpet.[56]
You entrust to the earth our bodies of earth
which you fashioned with your own hands
and you restore again what you have given,
transforming with incorruptibility and grace
what is mortal and deformed in us.[57]
You redeemed us from the curse and from sin,
having become both on our behalf.[58]
You have crushed the heads of the serpent[59]
who had seized man in his jaws
because of the abyss of our disobedience.
You have opened up for us a path
to the resurrection,
having broken down the gates of hell[60]
and reduced to impotence
the one who had power over death.[61]
You have given to those who fear you
a visible token,[62] the sign of the holy cross,
for the destruction of the Adversary
and for the protection of our life.

God Eternal,

ave cast myself from my mother's womb,[63]

ꞃ soul has loved[64] with all its strength,

n I have consecrated flesh and soul

my infancy up to this moment,

Put down beside me a shining angel

to lead me by the hand to the place of refreshment

where is the water of repose[65] near the lap of the holy fathers.[66]

You who have cut through the flame

of the fiery sword[67] and brought to paradise

the man who was crucified with you,

who entreated your pity,

remember me also in your kingdom,[68]

for I too have been crucified with you,[69]

for I have nailed my flesh out of reverence for you

and have feared your judgements.[70]

Let not the dreadful abyss[71] separate me

from your chosen ones.

Let not the Slanderer[72] stand against me on my journey.

Let not my sin be discovered before your eyes

if I have been overcome in any way

because of our nature's weakness

and have sinned in word or deed or thought.

You who have on earth the power to forgive sins,[73]

forgive me, so that I may draw breath again[74]

and may be found before you

in the stripping off of my body[75]

without stain or blemish[76] in the beauty of my soul,

but may my soul be received

blameless and immaculate into your hands

as an incense offering before your face."[77]

And as she spoke this prayer, she traced the sign of the cross on her eyes, her mouth and her heart. And little by little her tongue was burned dry by the fever and was no longer able to articulate her words, her voice was wavering and only by the parting of her lips and the movement of her hands did we recognise that she was praying.

Meanwhile, evening had come on and a light had been brought in. At once Macrina opened her eyes wide, directed their attention to the gleam of light and made it clear that she also wished to say the evening prayer of thanksgiving; but as her voice failed her, she realised her desire in her heart and in the movement of her hands, her lips moving in time with her inward impulse. When she had completed the prayer of thanksgiving and, by bringing her hand to her face for the sign of the cross, had indicated that she had finished her prayer, she took a strong, deep breath, and with that she died.

When from then on she did not breathe or move, I remembered the instructions she had given me when I had first arrived. She had said that she wished my hands to be placed upon her eyes and that she wanted me to attend to the customary care of the body. So I put my hand, numbed by grief, to her holy face at least so as not to seem to disregard her instruction. For her eyes needed no arranging, since they were covered gracefully by her eyelids as if she were only asleep; and her lips were firmly closed and her hands rested naturally on her breast, and the whole position of her body was so spontaneously and beautifully harmonised that any hand to compose the features was superfluous.

For two reasons my soul was distraught, both because of what I was actually seeing before my eyes and because of the wailing and weeping of the maidens which was resounding all around me. For, up to this point, they had continued to bear their suffering in silence and had kept in check the grief in their souls, stifling the impulse to cry out their sorrow because of the respect they had for her, as if they feared the reproach of her face even though it was now silent, in case some cry should break forth from them, against her command, and she, their teacher, be distressed by it. But when their suffering could no longer be contained in silence, and their grief was like a fire within them smouldering away at their souls, all at once a bitter, uncontrollable wailing erupted, with the result that my reason no longer maintained its proper balance; but, as if submerged by some winter-swollen river in flood, I was swept away by sorrow and, disregarding the tasks at hand, gave myself over entirely to lamentation. Besides, the maidens' grief seemed to me to have a just and reasonable cause. For they were not bewailing the loss of some ordinary acquaintance or physical attachment or any other similar relationship in which human beings find tragedy hard to bear, but it was as if they had been cut off from their hope in God and from the salvation of their souls; and so they cried out and wailed in high keening tones;

> The lamp of our eyes has been extinguished; the light to guide our souls has been carried off; our life's security dissolved; the seal of incorruptibility taken away; the bond of our community torn down; the support of the powerless crushed; the care of the weak taken away. With you even the night was illumined like day for us by your pure life. But now even the day will be changed to utter darkness.

From the girls who called her by the name of mother and nurse their grief flared out more passionately than from the rest. They were those who had been left prostrate along the roadways at the time of the famine; and she had picked them up, nursed them, brought them back to health and guided them personally to the pure, uncorrupted life.

But when I somehow gathered my soul back from some abyss, as it were, gazing intently at that holy head and, as though rebuked for the women's wild, noisy keening, I shouted loudly to the maidens: "Look at her and remember the precepts she taught you, that you conduct yourselves in an orderly and graceful fashion in every circumstance. One proper occasion for our tears her divine soul prescribed when she bade us weep only at the time of prayer. This is what we can also do now by changing wails of lamentation into a united singing of the psalms." I said this in a raised voice so as to make myself heard above the noise of their wailing.

Then I bade them retire for a little while to the house nearby, but I asked some of them to stay behind, those whose service she had been pleased to accept during her lifetime. Among them was a woman distinguished for her wealth, birth, the beauty of her body and much admired in her youth for her other accomplishments. She had been married to a man of high standing and after having lived with him for a short time, she was released from their union while she was still young. She had made the great Macrina the guardian and guide of her widowhood, and she lived for a long time with the maidens, learning the life of virtue from them. Her name was Vetiana, and her father, Araxios, was a member of the Senate. I told her that now at any rate there was no reproach in putting brighter clothing on the body and in decking out that pure, unsullied flesh in shining linens. She replied that we should find out what the holy one had judged to be proper, for it would not be right for us to do something which would not have been pleasing to her; but there was no question that what was dear and well-pleasing to God was also in harmony with Macrina's heart.

There was also a deaconess, in charge of a group of the women,[78] called Lampadion. She said that she knew exactly what Macrina had decided about her burial. And when I asked her about this, for she happened to be there when we were deciding what to do, she replied in tears and this is what she said: "The adornment of concern to the holy one was the pure life; this is for her both the ornament of her life and the shroud of her death. As to all those things which are for the ornamentation of the body, she neither had anything to do with them during her lifetime nor did she put any away for the present occasion, so that not even if we wanted to, would there be anything more than what we have here to dress her in."

"But isn't it possible," I asked, "to find something in the store cupboards with which we can adorn the bier?"

"In what store cupboards?" she replied. "You have in your hands everything she put away. Look at her cloak, look at the veil on her head, the worn sandals on her feet; this is her wealth, this her fortune! Apart from what you see there is nothing laid by in hidden chests or chambers in reserve. She knew only one repository for her own wealth, the treasury of heaven.[79] There she stored everything, and left nothing behind on earth."

"In that case," I said to her, "what if I brought one of the things I had prepared for the funeral,[80] would this be against her wishes?"

She replied that she did not think that Macrina would have disapproved of this. "For while she was still alive," she said, "she would have accepted such an honour from you for two reasons, because of your priesthood, which was always an honour for her, and because of your kinship; for she would not have considered alien to herself what belonged to her brother. For this reason too she commanded that her body be laid out by your own hands."

When this had been decided and it was necessary for that holy body to be clothed in fine linen, we shared out our responsibility and we were each of us around her concentrating on a different task. I for my part told one of my own company to bring me the robe.

Vetiana, of whom I spoke before, was arranging that holy head with her own hands when, putting her hand to Macrina's neck, she looked at me and said, "See what a necklace the holy woman wore for ornament."

And as she said this, she untied the chain from behind Macrina's neck, reached out her hand and showed me a cross of iron and a ring of the same material, both of which were hung on a slender chain and had been a always over her heart.

And I said, "Let this be our common possession. You keep the cross for your protection; the ring will be sufficient inheritance for me." And in fact the cross was engraved on the seal of the ring.

The woman looked intently at it and again spoke to me, "Your choice of this piece has not missed the mark; for the stone in the ring is hollow and in it is hidden a fragment of the wood of life;[81] and so the seal with its own engraving reveals from above what is hidden below."

When it was finally time to wrap her pure body in the robe, and the great Macrina's command made it necessary for me to perform this office, the woman who had shared with me in that important inheritance of Macrina's possessions was there helping out with the work.

"Do not let the greatest wonder accomplished by this holy lady," she said, "pass by unrecorded."

"What is that?" I asked.

She laid bare a part of Macrina's breast and asked. "Do you see this faint, tiny mark below the skin? It looks life a scar left by a small needle." And as she spoke she brought the lamp closer to the spot she was showing me. "What is so marvelous about that if the body has a tiny scar here?"

"This is left on the body," she said, "as a reminder of God's great help. For at one time on this spot there was a painful growth, and it was just as dangerous to cut out the tumour as it was to let it take its own course entirely without treatment with the risk that it would spread to the heart area. Her mother begged and entreated her many times to accept medical treatment, for she argued that this art too had been revealed by God for the saving protection of mankind. But Macrina had decided that to bare a part of her body to the eyes of strangers was worse than being sick, and one evening, when she had completed the tasks which she usually performed with her own hands for her mother, she went into the sanctuary and remained there all night long prostrate before the God of healing, weeping a flood of tears to moisten the earth, and she used the mud from her tears as a salve to put on the affected place. Her mother was at her wits end and again tried to get her to see the doctor, but Macrina said that it would be enough to cure her disease if her mother would make the sign of the cross with her own hand on Macrina's breast. And when her mother put her hand inside Macrina's robe to make the sign of the cross on the affected spot, the sign of the cross worked and the affliction disappeared.

"But this little mark," she continued, "appeared also at the time in place of the horrible tumour and stayed there till the end to be a reminder, I think, of God's visitation, as an impetus and cause for constant thanksgiving to God."

When our task was finished and the body adorned with the means at our disposal, the deaconess again told me that it was not right for Macrina to be seen by the maidens dressed as a bride.

"But I have a dark cloak of your mother's," she said, "which I think would be good to put over her so that this sacred beauty should not be made to shine in clothing brought in just for the occasion." Her view prevailed and the cloak was placed over the body. She shone even in the dark mantle; God's power, I think, added even such grace to her body that, exactly as in the vision I had while dreaming, rays of light seemed to shine out from her beauty.

While we were busy with these matters and the maidens' psalm-singing, mingled with lamentation, echoed all around the place, I do not know how but the news of her death had spread like wildfire throughout the surrounding area and all the people who dwelled round about began to flood in to witness the sad event, so that the vestibule was no longer big enough to hold the assembled people.

So we spent the whole night singing hymns around her body, just as they do in celebrating the deaths of martyrs,[82] and when dawn came, the crowds of both men and women who had flocked together from all the neighbouring districts were interrupting the singing of the psalms with their loud cries of grief.

But although my soul was distressed by the sad event, nonetheless I continued to reflect how it was possible, with the means I had at my disposal, not to omit anything which should be done on such an occasion; and so I separated the men from the women in the flood of people there, and put all the women in the choir with the maidens and the men in the ranks of the monks; thus I managed to get from the two groups a rhythmical, harmonious unity in their singing of the psalms, just as in proper choral singing, a beautifully ordered blend because of the shared responses of all.

And as the day advanced a little and the whole place round about her remote dwelling was packed tight with the crowds of people flooding in, the bishop of the region, who was called Araxios (for he was there with the full complement of his clergy), proposed that the body be brought forward immediately, since, as he noted, there was a fair distance to travel and the crowd would get in the way of the procession going any faster; and at the same time as he said this, he also ordered all the priests participating with him to escort the body themselves.

When this had been decided and the business was in hand, I went down by the bier and invited the bishop too to stand on the other side. Two other distinguished clergy took up their station at the opposite end of the bier and I led the way slowly, as was fitting, and little by little we moved off in procession. For the people were pressed in around the bier and nobody could see enough of that holy spectacle; consequently, there was no open ground for us to make our way easily. On either side of the body a large group of deacons and attendants led the way in rows, all with candles in their hands; and it was as if a liturgical procession was taking place,[83] since from beginning to end the psalms were sung beautifully in unison, as in the canticle of the three children.[84]

It was about seven or eight stadia[85] from the remote monastery to the church of the Holy Martyrs, where the bodies of our parents were also laid to rest, but it took just about all day for us to cover that distance, and not easily either. For the crowd which walked along with us and which was always getting bigger did not permit the procession to go off as we had planned. So when we were inside the doors of the church, we put the bier down and immediately turned to prayer; but the prayer was an invitation to the people to start their lamentations.

For there was silence after the singing of the psalms and when the maidens looked at that holy face, and our parents' tomb, where it had been decided to bury her, was already being opened, one of them shouted out distractedly that we would never again look upon that godlike face, and immediately the rest of the maidens shouted out with her just as wildly, and hopeless confusion drowned out our previous good order and the holy quality of the psalm singing, since everyone was weeping in response to the wailing of the maidens. It was with some difficulty that we signalled for silence. The master of ceremonies guided the people to prayer by intoning the customary prayers of the church, and they settled down into the position for prayer.

When the formal prayer was completed, a fear of the divine command forbidding one to unveil the shame of father or mother[86] came over me.

"How," I asked, "will be free of such condemnation if I look at the common shame of human nature in the bodies of my parents, since they can only be decomposed and disintegrated and changed into a hideous, repulsive formlessness?"

As I considered this, and Noah's anger against his son[87] was increasing my fear, the story of Noah showed me what I should do.[88] As they lifted the lid, before we were able to see the bodies, these were covered with a clean linen cloth which stretched from one side to the other; and so after the bodies were hidden under the cloth, we lifted up that holy body from the bier, both I and the local bishop I mentioned, and laid it down beside our mother, fulfilling a prayer shared by both of them; for they had both agreed throughout their lives in asking God for this, that after death their bodies should be reunited and that the partnership which they enjoyed while they lived should not be dissolved even in death.

When we had completed all the customary funeral rites and it was necessary to go back, I fell upon the tomb and kissed the dust and then took my way back again, downcast and tearful at the thought of how my life had been deprived of such a good.

Along the way, a distinguished military man who had command of a garrison in a little town of the district of Pontus, called Sebastopolis, and who lived there with his subordinates, came with kindly intention to meet me when I arrived there. He had heard of our misfortune and he took it badly (for, in fact, he was related to our family by kinship and also by close friendship). He gave me an account of a miracle worked by Macrina; and this will be the last event I shall record in my story before concluding my narrative. When we had stopped weeping and were standing in conversation, he said to me, "Hear what a great good has departed from human life." And with this he started to tell his story.

"It happened that my wife and I once desired to visit that power-house[89] of virtue; for that's what I think that place should be called in which the blessed soul spent her life. Our little daughter was also with us and she suffered from an eye ailment as a result of an infectious disease. And it was a hideous and pitiful sight, since the membrane around the pupil was swollen and because of the disease had taken on a whitish tinge. As we entered that divine place, we separated, my wife and I, to make our visit to those who lived a life of philosophy therein, I going to the monks' enclosure where your brother, Peter, was abbot, and my wife entering the convent to be with the holy one. After a suitable interval had passed, we decided it was time to leave the monastery retreat and we were already getting ready to go when the same, friendly invitation came to us from both quarters. Your brother asked me to stay and take part in the philosophic table,[90] and the blessed Macrina would not permit my wife to leave, but she held our little daughter in her arms and said that she would not give her back until she had given them a meal and offered them the wealth of philosophy; and, as you might have expected, she kissed the little girl and was putting her lips to the girl's eyes, when she noticed the infection around the pupil and said, "If you do me the favour of sharing our table with us, I will give you in return a reward to match your courtesy." The little girl's mother asked what it might be and the great Macrina replied, "It is an ointment I have which has the power to heal the eye infection." When after this a message reached me from the women's quarters telling me of Macrina's promise, we gladly stayed, counting of little consequence the necessity which pressed us to make our way back home.

Finally the feasting was over and our souls were full. The great Peter with his own hands[91] had entertained and cheered us royally, and the holy Macrina took leave of my wife with every courtesy one could wish for. And so, bright and joyful, we started back home along the same road, each of us telling the other what had happened to each as we went along. And I recounted all I had seen and heard in the men's enclosure, while she told me every little thing in detail, like a history book, and thought that she should omit nothing, not even the least significant details. On she went telling me about everything in order, as if in a narrative, and when she came to the part where a promise of a cure for the eye had been made, she interrupted the narrative to exclaim, "What's the matter with us! How did we forget the promise she made us, the special eye ointment?" And I was angry at our negligence and summoned some one to run back quickly to ask for the medicine, when our baby, who was in her nurse's arms, looked, as it happened, towards her mother. And the mother gazed intently at the child's eyes and then loudly exclaimed with joy and surprise, "Stop being angry at our negligence! Look! There's nothing missing of what she promised us, but the true medicine with which she heals diseases, the healing which comes from prayer, she has given us and it has already done its work, there's nothing whatsoever left of the eye disease, all healed by that divine medicine!" And as she was saying this, she picked the child up in her arms and put her down in mine. And then I too understood the incredible miracles of the gospel, which I had not believed in, and exclaimed: "What a great thing it is when the hand of God restores sight to the blind, when today his servant heals such sicknesses by her faith in Him, an event no less impressive than those miracles!"" All the while he was saying this, his voice was choked with emotion and the tears flowed into his story. This then is what I heard from the soldier.

All the other similar miracles which we heard about from those who lived with her and who knew in detail what she had done I do not think it prudent to add to our narrative. For most people judge the credibility of what is told them by the yardstick of their own experience, and what goes beyond the power of the hearer, this they have no respect for, suspecting that it is false and outside of the truth. For this reason I pass over that incredible farming miracle at the time of the famine, how the grain was distributed according to need and showed no sign of diminishing, how the volume remained the same both before it was given out to those who asked for it and after the distribution, and other miracles still more extraordinary, the cure of sicknesses, the casting out of demons, true prophecies of things to come; all of these are believed to be true by those who knew the details of them, even if they are beyond belief. But for those who are more bound to this world of flesh, they are considered to be outside the realm of what can be accepted, that is by those who do not know that the distribution of graces is in proportion to one's faith,[92] abundant for those who have in them a lot of room for faith.

In order therefore that those who have too little faith, and who do not believe in the gifts of God, should come to no harm, for this reason I have declined to make a complete record here of the greater miracles, since I think that what I have already said is sufficient to complete Macrina's story.

TEXTS AND TRANSLATIONS

EDITIONS

Gregorii Nysseni Opera Ascetica, ed. Virginia Woods Callahan in *Gregorii Nysseni Opera,* ed. Werner Jaeger, Vol. 8/1 (Leiden: E.J. Brill, 1952): pp. 347–414. This is the edition upon which I have largely based my translation, although I have occasionally followed Maraval's edition when it was clearly superior:

Grégoire de Nysse: Vie de Saint Macrine, introduction, texte critique, traduction, notes et index par Pierre Maraval, Sources chrétiennes 178 (Paris: Cerf, 1971).

Patrologia Graeca 46, cols. 960–1000.

TRANSLATIONS

Saint Gregory of Nyssa: Ascetical Works, The Fathers of the Church: A New Translation 58 (Washington. Catholic University of America Press, 1967).

Grégoire de Nysse: Vie de Saint Macrine, introduction, texte critique, traduction, notes et index par Pierre Maraval, Sources chrétiennes 178 (Paris: Cerf, 1971).

NOTES

1. *Vita Sanctae Macrinæ* (hereafter VSM).

2. For an excellent account and for the problem of the number of children in the family of Macrina and Gregory, see the introduction by M. Aubineau, *Traité de la virginité,* Sources chrétiennes 119 (Paris: Cerf, 1966) 21–82.

3. See, for example, *In laudem Basilii Magni,* PG 36, 505A, *In laudem Fratris Basilii,* PG 46, 808B and in Aubineau (see n. 2) 37.

4. On this, see Maraval, Introduction 45–46.

5. See *S. Pachomii Vita Bonhairice Scripta,* ed. L. Th. Lefort (Paris 1925) 26–28; *Vita S. Antonii* 54 (PG 26, col. 921); and generally J. Laporte, *The Role of Women in Early Christianity* (New York, Toronto, 1982) 77–81.

6. See the evidence collected by Maraval, Introduction 53–54, n. 3.

7. See Aubineau (n. 2 above), esp. 73–74.

8. On this, see R. Albrecht, *Das Leben der heiligen Makrina auf dem Hintergrund der Thekla-Traditionen* (Gottingen 1986); P. Wilson-Kastner, "Macrina: Virgin and Teacher," *St. Andrews University Seminary Series* 17 (Spring 1979) 105–118.

9. κατ᾿ εὐχήν: "to fulfill a vow" (Woods Callahan); "à la suite d'un vœu" (Maraval) and so all translators except Pasquali, "to fulfill a desire": "per adempiare un desiderio" ("Le Lettere di Gregorio di Nissa," *Studi Italiani di Filologia Classica,* Nuova Serie 3 (Florence, 1923) 118.

10. The ideal of philosophy (see also Introduction, part 3) as the ideal of the Christian monastic life plays a central role in the VSM and will undoubtedly seem strange, even alien, to modern ears

long accustomed to the departmentalisation and secularisation of academic disciplines. However, the essential and organic unity of the spiritual, intellectual and physical ways of life, central to the monastic *Rule of St. Basil,* will even yield such a remarkable phrase in the VSM as "the philosophic table." Nonetheless, this Christian usage reflects accurately not only the etymological meaning of the term "philosophy," i.e., love of wisdom, but also something of the original Socratic passion for the truth and care of the soul which are associated with the religious thirst of the sixth century B.C. in Greece and its aftermath, and especially with the inspired figures of Socrates himself and of Plato. The VSM makes reference to, and should be read together with, a philosophical conversation or dialogue between Macrina and Gregory on the nature of the soul and the resurrection: *De Anima et Resurrectione.* The VSM and *De Anima* together implicitly present a portrait of Macrina as the Christian Socrates, matching Plato's early Socratic dialogues about the nature of the soul and its inherent immortality, especially the Phaedo, Socrates' famous conversation with his friends on the day of his death. Socrates, like Macrina, presents arguments to support and explain his views, but Plato also makes it clear by the very drama of the dialogue that, when all is said and done, it is the choice of lives here and now which we must all confront if we are to realise the living, shining reality of the beautiful "soul" before us: Socrates in the *Phaedo,* Macrina in the VSM and *De Anima,* we may suggest. Hence, the ideal of philosophy for Plato – as indeed for all the ancients – was never something abstract or indeed remote, but the search for a living wisdom which involved the conversion of the whole person to the Good. A similar spirit invigorates Gregory's use of the term. There is of course, however, a great difference between the Platonic view of the *Phaedo,* which spurns the body, and that of Gregory in the VSM and *De Anima,* which spurns attachment to material things and therefore espouses separation of soul from body to this degree while, on the other hand, recognising that the body will be restored to its true God-created stature by the resurrection. On the tension between these different points of view in Gregory of Nyssa, see H. Cherniss, *The Platonism of Gregory of Nyssa* (Berkeley, 1930); J. Daniélou, *Platonisme et théologie mystique: Essai sur la doctrine spirituelle de Saint Grégoire de Nysse.* 2nd ed. (Paris, 1954); D.L. Balas, *Metousia Theou: Man's Participation in God's Perfections According to St. Gregory of Nyssa* (Rome, 1966), esp. 139–140, 150–152; D.L. Balas, "The Unity of Human Nature in Basil's and Gregory of Nyssa's Polemics Against Eunomius" *Studia Patristica* 14, pt. 3, ed. E.A. Livingstone (Berlin, 1976) 275–281. For a comparison with Socrates, see P. Wilson-Kastner, "Macrina: Virgin and Teacher."

11. The time of the persecutions is generally thought to have been between 306 and 317.

12. The mother's name was Emmelia. Her father had been put to death by an emperor, perhaps Licinius.

13. ὑπερήνθηει ... δὲ τῇ ὥρα τοῦ σώματος we might have substituted "beauty" for body in the translation here, but "body" reflects the original more accurately.

14. Thekla is the legendary virgin, disciple and helper of St. Paul whose deeds are recounted in the apocryphal *Acts of Paul and Thekla.* See R.A. Lipsius, *Acta apostolorum apocrypha.* Vol. 1 (Leipzig, 1891) 235–272; English translation in Edgard Hennecke, *New Testament Apocrypha,* ed. W. Schneemelcher, trans. R. McL. Wilson. Vol. 2 (Philadelphia, 1965) 353–364. For the Thekla tradition, see Introduction, section 3 as well as Wilson-Kastner, "Macrina: Virgin and Teacher" and Albrecht, *Das Leben der heiligen Makrina.*

15. I read καὶ μαρτυράμενον (Jaeger's correction of μαρτυρο-

μενον], which seems to make the best sense in this context.

16. Here, as elsewhere (*De An. et Res.,* PG 46, col. 17B; *De Virg.* 3, 10 f. 16=GN 8/1, 266, 2 f.=PG 46, col. 336C), Gregory demonstrates opposition to pagan culture. However, his writings also reveal a different attitude, permeated as they are, by a natural feeling and sense of respect for the highest elements of that culture (see e.g. especially *Epist.* 12, 4–6, GN 8/2, 45, 15–46, 12=PG 46, cols. 1048C– 1049A). A similar complex attitude is evident in the works of St. Augustine (cf. *De Civ. Dei* 2, 8, 62 with *Confess.* 3, 6, 11). And one might even see in Plato himself a double attitude. Despite the condemnation of profane myth and poiesis in general in *Republic* 2–3, 10 and *Laws* 7, the *Ion* presents a different view of art and, in the *Symposium,* Socrates is at the very end discussing the possibility of philosophical poetry, both tragedy and comedy. Gregory's attitude here, therefore, is not just a "Christian" view but is symptomatic of a deeper problem, probably felt at all times and place. See further J. Daniélou, *Grégoire de Nysse: La Vie de Moïse,* 3rd ed. (Paris, 1968). 31–88.

17. Here Gregory has in mind the unrestrained passionate power of the great, traditional heroines such as Clytemnestra, Medea, Electra, Phaedra and, of course, the Bacchic women. There is, however, among the Fathers a traditional distinction between "manly courage" (ἀνδρεία, virtus) and "feminine" lack of restraint (cf. below 969M = 380 W, p. 9; δυσγενές τι καὶ γυναικεῖον); and the two elements were, from the time of Aristotle, related respectively to "form" and "matter." This way of thinking, so foreign and distasteful to our own sensibility, should be balanced here by the consideration that it is Macrina, above all others in this powerful account, who not only transcends such oppositions, but also points to a thinking which will be able to reverse them, and learn thereby. On this theme

generally, see Albrecht, *Das Leben d. heiligen Makrina,* 197 ff.

18. I prefer to read τας αἰτίας to αἰσχύνας ("the shameful activities of the immoral characters"(Woods Callahan, 165) – τον κακον, lit. "of the evil things" or "people") for the simple reason that it is less acerbic. There is, however, no doubt that Gregory could have written αἰσχύνας.

19. With Woods Callahan I translate ταύτης πλέον "after this." In view of μαλίστα ("above all") immediately above, this seems to make more sense than Maraval's "de préférence" (cf. the Latin translation in Migne).

20. The word "moral," like the word "virtue," can sometimes have unfortunate connotations for the modern reader. The Greek ἠθικόν (like the Greek word ἀρετή, translated through the Latin as "virtue" but often better rendered as "excellence") did not possess these connotations for Gregory. Detachment or self-renunciation was certainly an important aspect of the Christian life and also of the Platonic tradition. But also important was the sense that the true moral/ethical life was not the rejection of any other "department" of reality but rather a dynamic and organic entrance into the God-given potential of life and nature. The "moral life," therefore, unifies the scattered elements of existence and helps to make even this world more real in the light of God's grace, not less.

21. Maraval compares Macrina's recitation of the psalter at specific times of the day with the Office of the day which Basil describes in a letter written in 358 to Gregory of Nazianzus (*Epist.* 2; PG 32, cols. 224–233). The two appear identical. However, the later *Rule of Basil* is much more detailed and developed. See Maraval, Introduction, 68–73 and 151, note 5.

22. lit. "of the elements themselves" (αὐτῶν τῶν στοιχείων). On this sense of στοιχεῖα, see A. Lampe, "Elementum" RLAC 4, cols. 1083–1084.

23. The notion of "Envy" (φθόνος), a personification of divine jealousy at any excess of happiness or talent among mortal beings, is originally a pagan Greek conception, but it is also frequently used by Christians of this period. Maraval cites many passages in both Gregory of Nyssa and Gregory Nazianzen (see generally 154–155, note 3). One major reason for this easy adoption of an essentially pagan image is that "Envy" is the envy of the devil who is the ultimate source of death in the world. On this, see also A. Louth, "Envy as the Chief Sin in Athanasius and Gregory of Nyssa" *Studia Patristica* 15, ed. E.A. Livingstone (Berlin, 1984) 458–460.

24. cf. Acts 23, 6.

25. Here I prefer to read πᾶσι (Maraval) instead of πᾶσαν (Woods Callahan) and to regard ἄλλοισ as pleonastic.

26. The more common reading (ἔχρισε: "when she had anointed her hands with mystic services," Woods Callahan, p. 167) has yielded three interpretations: 1) the practice of the day was to receive Communion in the hand; thus Macrina's hands were "anointed" by the reception of Communion for the rest of the day's tasks; 2) her hands were anointed in the sense that she prepared the breads for the Eucharist; 3) Macrina was a deaconess and her hands were "anointed" in this ministry. All these interpretations are discussed by Maraval (pp. 158–159, n. 2) and I concur with his judgement that the context would favour the reading ἔχρησε (a change merely of one letter, iota for eta), "lent her hands in service to the liturgies," surely the simpler and more straightforward reading in the circumstances. In other words, Macrina's first duty was the preparation of the Communion bread.

27. The three provinces are Pontus, Cappadocia and Armenia. On the question of whether Basil the Elder and Emmelia had nine or ten children, see J.E. Pfister, "A Biographical Note: The Brothers and Sisters of St. Gregory of Nyssa" *Vigiliae Christianae* 18 (1964)

108–113 and M. Aubineau, *Grégoire de Nysse: Traité de la virginité* (Paris, 1966) 35, n. 6. Maraval (186–187, n. 1) rejects the theory that one of the boys died young and makes the suggestion instead that in the VSM (973 M, 385 W) "les besoins du jeu de mots ont pu lui faire donner ce leger coup de pouce à la realité."

28. Immaterial (ἄυμλος), lit. "without matter," "not material." The term is broadly Platonic, but we should always be wary of reading too specific meanings into such terms, precisely because they are often common, as is the case here, to many different philosophical viewpoints simultaneously (e.g. Stoic, Peripatetic, Neoplatonic, etc.). Here, it seems to me, the primary connotations of αυλον are of a detachment from matter which is also a mastery over, and governance of, the material element in human composition.

29. On the sense in which γυναικεῖον should be understood, see n. 9 above.

30. λογισμοῖς, lit. "reasonings." In order to catch not only the narrower sense of reasoning or argument (here emphasised in an important way by Gregory as an integral part of the spiritual life), but also the more extended sense of rational reflection or meditation, either internal or with an interlocutor (as, for example, the whole series of reflections which are embedded in Macrina's arguments in her dialogue with Gregory on the soul, *De An. et Res.*), I have translated λογισμός as "reasoned reflection."

31. In the present context, the verb ἀποτινάξασθαι is probably reminiscent of Lk 9, 5.

32. That is, the normal preoccupations and tasks of this life were always subordinated to the spiritual life. This subordination of work to prayer is, of course, not an elimination of its necessity so much as a transformation of the focus of preoccupation.

33. cf. 1 Thes 5:17.

34. For the use of μεθόριος and the notion of "living at the

boundaries of human nature" in Gregory, see J. Daniélou, "Methorios: La notion de confins chez Grégoire de Nysse" *Recherches de Science Religieuse* 16 (1961) 161–187. The idea expressed here is very much related to the Neoplatonic notion of the soul as the intermediary between the Intelligible world of the Divine Mind (νοῦς and the κόσμος νοητός) and the physical world of the form-image in matter (κόσμος αἰσθητός). Certainly in the lines which follow, there is a marked contrast between transcendent nature, freed from passions, and human nature's continued "appearance" in the body. Here, however, we should see not simply the question of a Platonic separation of soul from body, but rather the spiritual drama of the person or self, even in this life. This, after all, is the spiritual drama that we find in Plato's presentation of Socrates in the *Phaedo* (see n. 2). The notion of being "at the boundaries" of human existence is also implicit in the (Pauline) images of the athlete and the race which Gregory employs here, and frequently elsewhere in his writings.

35. Here the spiritual "lightness" of soul is contrasted with the "material pull" of the body (οὐκ ἐβαροῦντο τῷ ἐθολκίῳ τοῦ σώματος). The participle, summetewroporou`sa, is a neologism based upon Plato's *Phaedrus* 246c (μετεωροπορεῖ). For the earlier pagan history of these spatial notions (especially in Plotinus) and for the view that they are often already integrated with key Aristotelian notions within a more comprehensive philosophical viewpoint, see my "Body's Approach to Soul: An Examination of a Recurrent Image in the *Enneads*" *Dionysius* 9 (1985) 37–52.

36. Here again we can see that philosophy is neither an abstraction nor even a personification in Gregory's thought, so much as the living reality of wisdom and of God's indwelling grace which grants increase to every human effort.

37. ἐπίνοια is difficult to translate. Woods Callahan's "foresight" is tempting, but I prefer to retain the more general connotations of the word. Foresight would be only one quality, among others, of Peter's genius for agriculture, handicraft, management, etc. The famine is probably to be dated to 368–369.

38. Basil was elected bishop of Caesarea in 370 and died on the 1st of January 379.

39. For the image, see Wis. 3:6; Prv. 17:3. Maraval (180, n. 1) also cites *Or. Cat.* 26, 6–7 (PG 45, col. 69A) and *De An. et Res.* (PG 46, col. 100A) where the image is used to illustrate the healing of humanity by Christ.

40. That is, the Arians. In these years, especially during the reign of the emperor Valens (who died in 378), it was not the easiest task to be a prominent public figure. For example, Gregory was expelled by an Arian dominated synod in 376 after being accused of financial mismanagement and the place in which he took refuge had had its Arian bishop expelled in a not unsimilar fashion. The most conspicuous example of the age was St. Athanasius who was recurrently exiled from the patriarchy of Alexandria. See *The Cambridge Mediaeval History*, Vol. 1, 118–142.

41. The two enclosures were situated quite close to one another and also close to a village on the same side of the river. Basil's monastery (perhaps originally the retreat of Naucratios) was situated on a hill on the opposite bank of the river. The two customs indicated here, the greeting by the community and the visit to the church before any other activity was undertaken, provide a vivid picture of the actual circumstances and spirit of early monastic life.

42. Gregory uses the term kaqhgoumevno- instead of the more frequent προεστώς; see Maraval p. 195, 5. J. Laporte (1982) identifies Lampadion, the deaconess, as "the head of the community" (87). R. Albrecht (1986) rightly points out that there is absolutely no basis

for this judgement in the text (50–51).

43. This is the long conversation recounted in the dialogue *De Anima et Resurrectione.*

44. The Greek of this passage is exceedingly difficult and the translations of Maraval and Woods Callahan reflect this. Maraval's "[il] ne permettait pas à sa sensibilité, grace à ses reflexions, de tomber dans la douleur" (for οὐ πρὸς τὸ ἀλγύνον τὴν αἴσθησιν τοῖς λογισμοῖς ἐπεκλίνετο) is bettered by Woods Callahan's "he did not direct attention to his pain" which catches the central point that it is a question of focus of attention or inclination of perception towards pain. But Woods Callahan's following translation "but kept the pain inside his body, neither blessing [misprint] his own activity. . . ." and Maraval's "tout en souffrant dans son corps, il ne laissait pas faiblir son activité propre" miss the force, *inter alia,* of ἐν . . . τῷ σώματι τὸ ἀλγοῦν εἶχεν. The question here is the control of consciousness, or of the focus of attention, and the background to the thought is the division of the human being into two selves: the lower, compound, bodily self and the higher self, the mind or intellectual soul which is ultimately impassible (free from corporeal effects). Here Gregory envisages a real distinction of faculties and signals this by his use of το; ἀλγοῦν and τὴν ἰδίαν ἐνέργειαν (translated here as "the faculty which felt the pain" and "his own proper activity" respectively). The mind, therefore, can be affected by bodily suffering if it gives its attention to the body and allows itself to be localised, so to speak, "in" the body. In its own nature, however, the mind or intellectual soul is not "in" the body at all in the same sense as an eye, a colour or a feeling is "in" the body. The mind is present to, or "in" the body in an altogether different sense, as the power of direction and control is present "in" something, and it can, therefore, recognise its distinction from what it controls, from that which experiences pain, and

continue uninterruptedly its own proper activity which is the higher life of thought and contemplation. Clearly it is the thought of Plotinus – or of Porphyry, Plotinus' pupil and disciple – which lies behind this passage. For Plotinus the true nature of the mind is divine and its true abode is with God. Of this we are, for the most part, unconscious, taking our particular focus of consciousness for the whole of reality. For an account of this, see *The Cambridge History of Later Greek and Early Mediaeval Philosophy,* ed. A.H. Armstrong (Cambridge, 1967), and for some precision on the relationship between Plotinus and Gregory see J. Daniélou, "Grégoire de Nysse et Plotin" in *Association G. Budé, Congrès de Tours et Poitiers 1953: Actes du Congrès* (Paris, 1954) 259–262; and A. Meredith, "Gregory of Nyssa and Plotinus" in *Studia Patristica* 17, pt. 3, ed. E.A. Livingstone (Oxford: Pergamon Press, 1982) 1120–1126. This passage also illustrates the pivotal role of the discursive reason, λογισμός: the reasoned reflection – or power of reasoning – in assenting or dissenting to the passions. The fact of suffering is not within our control but our attitude to suffering is voluntary and Job's control of his inclination inherently rational.

45. cf. Rm 6:11; 8:10.

46. cf. Rm 8:11.

47. cf. Phil 3:14.

48. 2 Tm 4:8.

49. 2 Tm 4:7.

50. ἐκ θείας Φιλανθρωπίας. This is a frequent theme elsewhere in Gregory's writings especially in relation to the Incarnation. For references, see Maraval, 206, n. 1.

51. cf. Acts 4:35, according to which any money received from the sale of land or houses was brought to the apostles, thence to be redistributed to those in need.

52. cf. Ps 118:48.

53. lit. "about," but Gregory here emphasises the object of choice for her whole life.

54. ἐν ἀπαθείᾳ here makes explicit what was implicit in Gregory's characterisation of Job above (see n. 36). On ἀπάθεια in Gregory, see J. Daniélou, *Platonisme et théologie mystique* (Paris, 1954), 92–103; W. Voelker, *Gregor von Nyssa als Mystiker* (Wiesbaden, 1955), 117–123.

55. cf. Heb 2:15.

56. cf. 1 Cor 15:52.

57. cf. 1 Cor 15:53.

58. cf. Gal 3:13 and 2 Cor 5:21.

59. cf. Ps 73:14.

60. cf. Ps 106:16 and Mt 16:18.

61. cf. Heb 2:14.

62. cf. Ps 59:16.

63. cf. Ps 21:11.

64. cf. Song 1:7.

65. cf. Ps 22:2. For refreshment, see Ps 65:12; 38:14.

66. cf. Lk 16:22.

67. cf. Gen 3:24.

68. cf. Lk 23:42–43.

69. cf. Gal 2:19.

70. cf. Ps 118:120.

71. cf. Lk 16:26.

72. βάσκανος is related in Gregory to φθόνος ("envy," see n. 15). On this, see Maraval, 224, n. 1.

73. cf. Mt 9:6; Mk 2:10.

74. cf. Ps 38:14.

75. cf. Col 2:11.

76. cf. Eph 5:27.

77. cf. Ps 140:2.

78. The "group of women," maidens or virgins (χορὸς τῆς παρθενίας). The group/choir of maidens" (τῷ τῶν παρθένων χορῷ, 993M, 407 w) below may well refer to a "choir" as J. Quasten thought: *Musik und Gesang in den Kulten der heidnischen Antike und christlichen Frühzeit* (Münster, 1930), 229; or it may simply be more general in application (as in, for example, *De Inst. Chr.*, GN 8/1, 41, 20–21: τὸν τῆς θιλοσοφίας χορόν). On the role of deaconesses, consult J. Laporte, *The Role of Women in Early Christianity* (New York, 1982) 109–132.

79. cf. Mt 6:19–20; 17:21.

80. Maraval translated "pour ma sepulture" which is possible but less likely in the context.

81. cf. Gen 3:24; Rv 2:7.

82. ἐπὶ μαρτύρων πανηγύρεως. For the term πανήγυρις (whence the English "panegyric"), see the references *ad loc.* in Bauer, *A Greek-English Lexicon of the New Testament and Other Early Christian Literature* and Lampe, *A Patristic-Greek Lexicon.*

83. For the sort of procession Gregory has in mind, as Maraval points out *ad loc.,* see his description of the Paschal vigil procession in *In Salut. Pasch.* (GN 9, 309, 9 f. =PG 46, col. 681C) and Gregory Nazianzus' description of the solemn entry of neophytes into the Church, in *Or.* 40 (*In Sanct. Bapt.*) 46 (=PG 36, 425B).

84. cf. Dan 3:51.

85. That is, about 1½ km.

86. cf. Lv 18:7.

87. cf. Gn 9, 25.

88. cf. Gn 9:23.

89. "Power-house" (φροντιστήριον), originally in Aristophanes' *Clouds* (94): the "think-tank," the satirical term for Socrates' school which nonetheless entered into proper usage. See,

for example, the entries in Liddell and Scott, *Greek-English Lexicon and Lampe, A Patristic-Greek Lexicon.* There is nonetheless a delightfully gentle humour running through the whole of this passage which serves to present a vivid, human picture of the soldier, his wife, and little girl.

90. For the comprehensive but nevertheless concrete and practical idea of philosophy which pervaded the monastic life, see n. 2 above.

91. Here I have followed Maraval: 1) ἡ ψυχή ("our souls were full") instead of Woods Callahan ἡ εὐχή ("grace was said"); and 2) ταῖς οἰκείαις χερσίν ("with his own hands") instead of χάρισιν ("with special graciousness"). χερσίν (2) seems necessary within the idiom of the VSM, ψυχή (1) much less so.

92. cf. Rm 12:6.

SELECT BIBLIOGRAPHY

Albrecht, Ruth. *Das Leben der heiligen Makrina auf dem Hintergrund der Thekla-Traditionen: Studien zu den Ursprungen des weiblichen Mönchtums im 4. Jahrhundert in Kleinasien* (Gottingen: Vandenhoeck & Ruprecht, 1986).

Balas, David L. *Metoysia Theoy: Man's Participation in God's Perfections according to St. Gregory of Nyssa* (Rome: Herder, 1966).

—"The Unity of Human Nature in Basil's and Gregory of Nyssa's Polemics Against Eunomius" *Studia Patristica* 14/3, ed. E. A. Livingstone (Berlin, 1976) 275–281.

Bardy, J., "Toute une famille de Sainte Macrine et ses frères" *Le Correspondant* (19 fevrier 1937) 273–286.

Cherniss, Harold, *The Platonism of Gregory of Nyssa* (Berkeley: University of California Press, 1934).

Corrigan, Kevin, "Body's Approach to Soul: An Examination of a Recurrent Image in the Enneads" *Dionysius* 9 (1985) 37–52.

Daniélou, Jean. "Grégoire de Nysse et Plotin," *Association G. Budé, Congrès de Tours et Poitiers 1953: Actes du Congrès* (Paris, 1954) 259–262.

—"Methorios: La notion de confins chez Grégoire de Nysse" *Recherches de Science Religieuse* 16 (1961) 161–187.

—*Platonisme et théologie mystique: Essai sur la doctrine spirituelle de Saint Grégoire de Nysse* (Paris: Aubier, 1944).

— "La resurrection des corps chez Grégoire de Nysse" *Vigiliae Christianae* 7 (1953) 154–170.

Ensslin, W. "Macrina" in *Realencyclopädie der klassischen Alterthums-Wissenschaft* 27, cols.168–169.

Festugière, A. J. "Lieux communs et thèmes de folklore dans l'hagiographie primitive" *Wiener Studien* 73 [Festschrift Johannes Mewalt] (1960) 123–152.

Frank, Suso. *Angelikos bios: Begriffsanalystische und begriffsgeschichtliche Untersuchung zum "engelgleichen Leben" im frühen Mönchtum,* Beitrag zur Geschichte des alten Mönchtums und des Benediktinerordens 26 (Münster: Aschendorff, 1964).

——"Vraisemblance psychologique et forme littéraire chez les anciens" *Philologus* 102 (1958) 21–42.

Goggin, Sister Thomas Aquinas. *The Times of Gregory of Nyssa as Reflected in the Letters and the Contra Eunomium* (Washington Catholic University of America, 1947).

Gregory of Nyssa. *Traité de la virginité,* introd., text1e crit., trad., comm. et index par Michel Aubineau, Sources chrétiennes 119 (Paris: Cerf, 1966).

——*La Vie de Moïse; ou, Traité de la perfection en matière de vertue,* introd., texte crit., et trad. par Jean Daniélou, Sources chrétiennes (Paris: Cerf, 1968).

——*The Life of Moses,* trans., introd. and notes by Abraham J. Malherbe and Everett Ferguson; pref. by John Meyendorff (New York: Paulist Press, 1978).

——*Vie de Sainte Macrine,* introd:, texte crit., trad., notes et index par Pierre Maraval, Sources chrétiennes 178 (Paris: Cerf, 1971).

Gribomont, J. "Le Panégyrique de la virginité; œuvre de jeunesse de Grégorie de Nysse" *Revue d'Ascétique et de Mystique* 48 (1967) 249–266.

Gryson, Roger. *The Minstry of Women in the Early Church* (Collegeville MN: Liturgical Press, 1976).

Jelphanion, G. de. "Ibora-Gazoura" Étude de géographie pontique" *Mélanges de la Faculté Orientale (Beyrouth)* 5/1 (1911) 333–354.

Kalsbach, A. "Vom Mensch- und Lebensideal der christlichen Antike: Gregors von Nyssa *Vita S. Macrinae*" in *Das Bild vom*

Menschen (Düsseldorf, 1934) 36–41.

Kloeppel, M. "Makrina die Jungere: eine altchristliche Frauengestalt" in Theodore Bogler, *Frauen in Bannkreis Christi* (Maria-Laach, 1964), 80–94.

Laporte, Jean. *The Role of Women in Early Christianity* (New York: E. Mellen, 1982).

Loofs, F. "Makrina die Jungere" in *Realencyclopädie für protestantische Theologie und Kirche* 12, cols. 93–94.

Louth, A. "Envy as the Chief Sin in Athanasius and Gregory of Nyssa" in *Studia Patristica* 15, ed. E.A. Livingstone (Berlin: Akademie-Verlag, 1984) 458–460.

Malingrey, A.M. *'Philosophia': Étude d'un groupe de mots dans la littérature grecque des présocratiques au IVe siècle après J.-C.* (Paris: Klincksieck, 1961).

Marotta, E. "La base biblica della *Vita S. Macrinae* di Gregorio di Nissa'" *Vetera Christianorum* 5 (1968) 73–88.

— "Similitudini ed ecphraseis nella *Vita S. Macrinae* di Gregorio di Nissa" *Vetera Christianorum* 7 (1970) 265–284.

Mateos, J. "L'office monastique à la fin du IVe siècle: Antioche, Palestine, Cappadoce" *Orientalis Christianae* 47 (1963) 53–88.

Meredith, A. "Gregory of Nyssa and Plotinus" in *Studia Patristica* 17/3, ed. E.A. Livingstone (Oxford: Pergamon Press, 1982) 1120–1126.

Metz, R. *La consécration des vierges dans l'église romaine: Étude d'histoire de la liturgie* (Paris: Presses Universitaires de France, 1954).

Pasquali, G. "Le Lettere di Gregorio di Nissa" *Studi Italiani di Filologia Classica (NS)* 3 (1923) 75–136.

Pfister, J.E. "The Brothers and Sisters of St. Gregory of Nyssa" *Vigiliae Christinae* 18 (1964) 108–113.

Quasten, J. *Musik und Gesang in den Kulten der heidnishen Antike und christlichen Frühzeit* (1930; rpt. Münster: Aschendorff, 1973).

Ramsay, W.M. *The Historical Geography of Asia Minor* (1890; rpt. New York: Cooper Square, 1972).

Venables, E. "Macrina the Younger" in *A Dictionary of Christian Biography,* ed. William Smith and Henry Wace. Vol. 3 (London: John Murray, 1882) 779.

Volker, W. *Gregor von Nyssa als Mystiker* (Wiesbaden: F. Steiner, 1955).

Wilson-Kastner, Patricia. "Macrina: Virgin and Teacher" *St. Andrews University Seminary Series* 17 (Spring 1979) 105–118.